Contents

Extreme mammals

Think you know everything about mammals? Think again! All mammals have hair or fur, and feed their babies with milk. But the differences between mammals are what make them **extreme**.

Most mammals live on land. A few live in the ocean, like this dugong.

Some mammals have bizarre bodies. Some behave in weird ways. These features help them to find **mates** or food – or avoid getting eaten themselves!

Prickly porcupines

Porcupines have **extreme** fur. Each of their **spines** is a giant, stiff hair. When a porcupine is scared, it raises and rattles its spines. It does this using the same muscles that give people goosebumps.

porcupine

If the **predator** doesn't run away, the porcupine has another trick. It runs backwards and pushes its prickly bottom into the attacker's face!

Nosy elephants

An elephant's trunk is an amazing tool. Elephants use them to:

- grab food
- suck up water to drink or wash
- **snorkel** underwater
- smell and breathe
- work out where other elephants are
- trumpet.

tusk

trunk

African elephants are the largest land mammals in the world.

9

Crafty camels

Bactrian camels survive in rocky deserts. There is little to eat and drink. The camel's lip collects snot that trickles out of its nose. The snot flows back into the camel's mouth, so no water is wasted!

humps store fat for energy

Camels swallow their food whole. Then they throw it up and chew it again to make it softer! This helps them **digest** very tough foods. Camels have eaten bones, rope, and even tents!

11

Bizarre bills

These weird mammals have soft, rubbery **bills**. They help platypuses to sense food. Using its bill, a platypus can hunt under water with its eyes closed.

bill

webbed feet for swimming

DID YOU KNOW?

Platypuses lay eggs, like reptiles. But their babies drink milk from their mothers, like other mammals. Milk oozes out of the mother's skin. The babies lick it off her fur.

Animal armour

A pangolin's body is covered in horny **scales** made from the same material as fingernails. When a pangolin is frightened, it rolls in a ball and flicks the scales out like blades.

scale

powerful claws
to dig for insects

DID YOU KNOW?
Some pangolins can squirt a stinky liquid from their bottoms. It smells so disgusting it can scare away tigers!

15

Touchy - feely moles

The star-nosed mole lives in dark underground tunnels. It explores the world through its nose. Weird tentacles around its nose give it the best sense of touch of any mammal.

huge claws for digging

tentacles

How good is your sense of touch? Close your eyes and see how long it takes you to work out what 12 objects are by touching them. It takes the star-nosed mole one second!

Flapping fingers

Bats are the only mammals that can fly. Their wings are actually skin stretched between very long fingers. Bats also have amazing hearing. Some bats can hear the sound of an insect walking on a leaf!

Terrible tigers

Tigers are the largest cats in the world. They are killing machines. Every part of their body is **adapted** for hunting meat. They can tackle enormous oxen and buffalo.

stripy coat for **camouflage**

long teeth for a deadly bite

DID YOU KNOW?
A tiger's stripes are like a human fingerprint. No two tigers have the same pattern.

Bright blue bottoms!

How do you spot the most important people in your school? Mandrills show who is boss by turning their bottoms bright blue and red! They are the most colourful mammals.

The strongest, most fearsome males have the brightest bottoms.

long teeth
for fighting

orange beard

23

Whale of a noise

Sperm whales make the loudest sound of any animal. Their booming clicks are as loud as a space rocket taking off. The sounds bounce off squid and fish. The **echo** tells the whale what and where the food is.

Right whales have the world's biggest mouths. But they eat some of the smallest food! They eat tiny animals from seawater.

Mighty munchers

A rodent's teeth never stop growing! This means they can chew through very hard things. Beavers can chomp through tree trunks. Rats can chew through lead and aluminium. Their teeth get damaged, but they quickly grow back.

beaver

DID YOU KNOW?

A rat's teeth grow 10 centimetres every year. If the rat can't find anything to **gnaw**, its teeth will grow through its skull.

Record-breakers

Which mammal do you think is the most **extreme**? Why? Have a look at some of these record-breaking mammals to help you decide.

What? Blue whale

Why? World's largest animal

Wow! Blue whales can grow to more than 30 metres long. Even their babies weigh 2–3 tonnes. That's as much as a car!

What? Cheetah

Why? World's fastest land animal

Wow! Cheetahs can reach top speeds of 87 kilometres an hour. That's as fast as a speeding car!

What? Spotted hyena

Why? Best at clearing their plate

Wow! Strong jaws and teeth mean these **scavengers** can eat bones, skin, hooves, and horns!

What? Rhinoceros

Why? World's thickest skin

Wow! The skin on a rhino's back can be 2.5 centimetres thick, which is about the length of a paperclip.

What? Giraffe

Why? Tallest animal

Wow! Males can grow up to six metres tall, or three times taller than a door!

What? Three-toed sloth

Why? World's slowest mammal

Wow! This mammal moves at just 0.24 kilometres an hour. That's only five times faster than a snail!

29

Glossary

adapted changed over time to become suited for a special purpose

bill hard mouth-part of a bird or other animal

camouflage colours or markings that help an animal to blend in with the things around it

echo sound caused by another sound bouncing off something

extreme unusual, amazing, or different from normal

digest break down food so that the body can use it

gnaw bite or chew on again and again

mates two animals that can have baby animals together

predator animal that hunts other animals for food

scales overlapping horny or bony plates that cover some animals' bodies

scavenger animal that finds and eats dead animals

snorkel tube that an animal uses to breathe through when its head is under water

spines sharp, pointed body parts that stick out on some animals

Find out more

Books

Crocodile vs Wildebeest (Predator vs Prey), Mary Meinking (Raintree, 2012)

Gorilla (Eye on the Wild), Suzi Eszterhas (Frances Lincoln Children's Books, 2012)

Killer Cats (Wild Predators), Andrew Solway (Raintree, 2005)

Websites

Watch videos of marvellous mammals and other animals:
kids.nationalgeographic.com/kids/animals/

See a pangolin in action:
www.bbc.co.uk/nature/life/ Pangolin#p00bdp28

Play wild games and read animal books online:
www.zsl.org/kids/

Index